CYBERSECURIT'

English-Spanish

This glossary is a compilation of more than 1,000 terms in English and their translation into Spanish related to the topic of security in cyberspace.

Terms within the following linguistic categories are included:

- Vocabulary on networking, information technology and telecommunications

- Specific terminology about cyberattacks or cybercrime

- Most common acronyms used in the field of cybersecurity

- Concepts about cryptography, cryptocurrencies, and mathematical algorithms

---

GLOSARIO DE CIBERSEGURIDAD

Español-Inglés

Este glosario es una compilación de más de 1.000 términos en español y su traducción al inglés relacionados con el tema de la seguridad en el ciberespacio.

Se incluyen términos dentro de los siguientes ámbitos:

- Vocabulario sobre redes informáticas, tecnología de la información y telecomunicaciones
- Terminología específica sobre ataques cibernéticos o ciberdelincuencia
- Principales acrónimos utilizados en el ámbito de la ciberseguridad
- Conceptos sobre criptografía, criptomonedas y algoritmos matemáticos

PART I: ENGLISH-SPANISH

A

AaaS (Access as a Service): AaaS (acceso como servicio)

Abuse: Abuso

Access: Acceso

Access attempt: Intento de acceso

Access code: Código de acceso

Access control: Control de acceso

Active attack: Ataque activo

Ad fraud (advertising fraud): Fraude publicitario

Advanced persistent threat (APT): Amenaza persistente avanzada (APT)

Adversary: Adversario

Advertising: Publicidad

Adware: Software publicitario (software que muestra anuncios)

AES (Advanced Encryption Standard): AES (estándar de cifrado avanzado)

Alert: Alerta

Altcoin (alternative coin): Altcoin (criptomoneda alternativa)

Anfitrión (host): Host

Anomaly: Anomalía

Anonymity: Anonimato

Anonymization (anonymisation): Anonimización

Anonymous: Anónimo/a

Anonymous user: Usuario anónimo

Antimalware: Antimalware (software antimalicioso)

Antispam: Antispam (protección contra correo no deseado)

Antispoofing: Antisuplantación

Antispyware: Antispyware (software antiespía)

Antivirus: Antivirus

ASR (Attack Surface Reduction): ASR (reducción de la superficie de ataque)

Assets: Activos

Asset tokenization: Tokenización de activos

Attachment: Archivo adjunto (datos adjuntos)

Attack (assault): Ataque

Attack signature: Firma del ataque

Attack vector: Vector de ataque

Attacker: Atacante

Authentication: Autenticación (autentificación)

Authentication authority: Autoridad de autenticación

Authentication policy: Política de autenticación

Authenticity: Autenticidad

Authority: Autoridad

Authorization: Autorización

Authorization data: Datos de autorización

Authorized user: Usuario autorizado

Autocryptography: Autoencriptación

Automatic recovery: Recuperación automática (autorrecuperación)

Automorphism: Automorfismo

Autorun worm: Gusano autoejecutable

Avalanche: Avalancha

Avoidance: Evitación (elusión)

B

B2B (Business to Business): B2B (negocio a negocio)

B2C (Business to Consumer): B2B (negocio a consumidor)

BaaS (Blockchain as a Service): BaaS (cadena de bloques como servicio)

Backup (backup copy): Copia de seguridad (copia de respaldo)

BadUSB (Rubber Ducky, bad beetle USB): USB malicioso (BadUSB)

Bait: Anzuelo

Bank account: Cuenta bancaria

Bank card: Tarjeta bancaria

Bank fraud: Estafa bancaria

Bank transfer (wire transfer): Transferencia bancaria

Bastion: Bastión

BCP (Business Continuity Plan): PCN (Plan de Continuidad de Negocio)

BEC (Business Email Compromise): BEC (compromiso de correo electrónico empresarial)

BIA (Business Impact Analysis): BIA (análisis de impacto de negocio)

Bitcoin: Bitcoin

Black box algorithm: Algoritmo de caja negra

Black hat hacker (malicious hacker, cracker): Hacker de sombrero negro (pirata, cracker)

Black list: Lista negra (lista de bloqueados)

Black market: Mercado negro

Blackmail: Chantaje

BlackNurse attack: Ataque BlackNurse

Blackout: Apagón

Blind certificate: Certificado ciego

Blind signature: Firma ciega

Block: Bloque

Block chaining: Encadenamiento de bloques

Block cipher: Cifrado de bloques

Blockchain: Cadena de bloques

Blocked sender: Remitente bloqueado

Blue hat hacker: Hacker de sombrero azul

Bluebugging: Bluebugging (forma de ataque Bluetooth)

Bluejacking: Bluejacking (envío de mensajes con Bluetooth)

Bluesnarfing: Bluesnarfing (ataque a través de Bluetooth)

Bombing: Bombardeo

Bot (robot, software robot): Bot (robot)

Botnet (robot network): Botnet (red de robots)

Breach (violation, infringement): Vulneración (violación, infracción)

Brute force: Fuerza bruta

Brute force attack: Ataque por fuerza bruta

Bulk e-mail: Correo masivo

Business continuity plan (BCP): Plan de continuidad de negocio (PCN)

C

CA (Certification Authority): CA (autoridad certificadora)

CaaS (Cybercrime as a Service): CaaS (cibercrimen como servicio)

Call recording: Grabación de llamada

CAPEC (Common Attack Pattern Enumeration and Classification): CAPEC (enumeración y clasificación de patrones de ataque comunes)

CAPTCHA (Completely Automated Public Turing test to tell Computers and Humans Apart): CAPTCHA (test público y completamente automatizado de Turing para diferenciar computadoras de humanos)

CAPTCHA test: Prueba de CAPTCHA

Card: Tarjeta

Card cryptogram: Criptograma de la tarjeta

Card reader: Lector de tarjetas

Carding: Estafa de las tarjetas bancarias

CASB (Cloud Access Security Broker): CASB (agente de seguridad de acceso a la nube)

Catfishing (catphishing): Catfishing (catphishing, impostura)

CAVP (Cryptographic Algorithm Validation Program): CAVP (programa de validación de algoritmos criptográficos)

CDO (Chief Data Officer): CDO (director/a de datos, DD)

CEO scam (CEO fraud, Chief Executive Officer fraud): Estafa del CEO (fraude del CEO, fraude del director ejecutivo)

CERT (Computer Emergency Response Team): CERT (equipo de respuesta ante emergencias informáticas)

Certificate: Certificado

Certificate of authenticity (COA): Certificado de autenticidad (COA)

Certificate policy: Política de certificados

Certification Authority (CA): Autoridad certificadora (CA)

Character set: Juego de caracteres

Chatbot (talkbot, voice assistant): Chatbot (asistente de voz, asistente virtual)

Check (cheking, verification): Comprobación

Checker: Comprobador

Checklist: Lista de comprobación

Chief data officer (CDO): Director/a de datos (DD)

Chief Executive Officer fraud (CEO fraud, CEO scam): Fraude del director ejecutivo (fraude del CEO, estafa del CEO)

Child grooming: Captación de menores (grooming)

Cipher (cypher): Cifra (clave, código, mensaje cifrado, mensaje codificado)

Cipher block chaining (CBC): Encadenamiento de bloques de cifrado

Cipher key: Clave de cifrado

Cipher system: Sistema de cifrado

Cipher text: Texto de cifrado

CISA (Cybersecurity and Infrastructure Security Agency): CISA (agencia de seguridad de infraestructura y ciberseguridad)

Classified: Clasificado/a (reservado/a)

Click fraud: Fraude del clic

Clickbait: Ciberanzuelo (cebo de clics)

Clickjacking: Secuestro de clics

Cloud: Nube

Cloud access security broker (CASB): Agente de seguridad de acceso a la nube (CASB)

Cloud app: Aplicación en la nube

Cloud computing: Computación en la nube (informática en la nube)

Cloud security posture management (CSPM): Gestión de la postura de seguridad en la nube (CSPM)

Cloudjacking: Cloudjacking (cryptojacking en la nube)

COA (Certificate Of Authenticity): COA (certificado de autenticidad)

Code: Código

Coin: Moneda

Combinatorics: Combinatoria

Common vulnerabilities and exposures (CVE): Vulnerabilidades y exposiciones comunes (CVE)

Compromise: Compromiso

Compromised: Comprometido/a

Compromised system: Sistema comprometido

Computer: Ordenador (computador/a, equipo)

Computer attack: Ataque informático

Computer emergency response team (CERT): Equipo de respuesta ante emergencias informáticas (CERT)

Computer security incidence response team (CSIRT): Equipo de respuesta ante incidencias de seguridad informática (CSIRT)

Computer virus: Virus informático

Confidential: Confidencial

Confidential data (sensitive data): Datos confidenciales

Confidentiality (secrecy): Confidencialidad

Configuration (settings, setup): Configuración

Confinement: Confinamiento

Consent: Consentimiento

Counterfeit: Falsificación (falso/a, falsificado/a)

Counterfeit money (fake money): Dinero falsificado (dinero falso, moneda falsa)

Counterfeit software: Software falsificado

Counterfeiting: Falsificación

Counter-signature: Contrafirma

CPS (Certification Practice Statement): CPS (declaración de prácticas de certificación)

Crack: Grieta

Cracker (black hat hacker): Pirata (pirata informático/a)

Cracking (software cracking, code cracking): Cracking (pirateo de software, descifrado)

CRC (Cyclic Redundancy Check): CRC (comprobación de redundancia cíclica)

Credential: Credencial

Criticality: Criticidad

Cross Site Request Forgery (CSRF): Falsificación de solicitud entre sitios (CSRF)

Cryptanalysis: Criptoanálisis

Cryptanalyst: Criptoanalista

Cryptoassets: Criptoactivos

Cryptocurrency: Criptomoneda (moneda criptográfica)

Cryptocurrency mining (cryptomining): Minería de criptomonedas (criptominería)

Cryptographic algorithm: Algoritmo criptográfico

Cryptographic algorithm validation program (CAVP): Programa de validación de algoritmos criptográficos (CAVP)

Cryptograhic system: Sistema criptográfico

Cryptogram: Criptograma

Cryptographer: Criptógrafo/a

Cryptography: Criptografía

Cryptojacking: Criptosecuestro

Cryptologist: Criptólogo/a

Cryptology : Criptología

Cryptominer: Criptominero/a

Cryptomining (cryptocurrency mining): Criptominería (minería de criptomonedas)

Cryptosystem (cryptograhic system): Criptosistema (sistema criptográfico)

Cryptovirology: Criptovirología

Cryptovirus: Criptovirus

Cryptowallet: Criptomonedero

CSIRT (Computer Security Incidence Response Team): CSIRT (equipo de respuesta ante incidencias de seguridad informática)

CSPM (Cloud Security Posture Management): CSPM (gestión de la postura de seguridad en la nube)

CSRF (Cross Site Request Forgery): CSRF (falsificación de solicitud entre sitios)

CTI (Cyber Threat Intelligence): CTI (inteligencia sobre ciberamenazas)

Customized attack: Ataque personalizado

CVE (Common Vulnerabilities and Exposures): CVE (vulnerabilidades y exposiciones comunes)

CVS (Common Vulnerability Scoring): CVS (puntuación vulnerabilidades comunes)

CWE (Common Weaknesses Enumeration): CWE (enumeración de debilidades comunes)

Cyber law: Ciberderecho

Cyberactivism (Internet activism): Ciberactivismo

Cyberanalist: Ciberanalista

Cyberattack: Ciberataque

Cybercafé (Internet café): Cibercafé

Cybercrime: Cibercrimen (delito cibernético, ciberdelito)

Cybercrime as a Service (CaaS): Cibercrimen como servicio (CaaS)

Cybercriminal: Ciberdelincuente

Cyberculture: Cibercultura

Cyber-espionage (cyberspying): Ciberespionaje

Cyberexercice: Ciberejercicio

Cybermule (money mule): Cibermula

Cybernaut: Cibernauta

Cybernetics: Cibernética

Cybersabotage: Cibersabotaje

Cyberscam (online scam): Ciberestafa (estafa en línea)

Cybersecurity: Ciberseguridad

Cybersecurity and Infrastructure Security Agency (CISA): Agencia de seguridad de infraestructura y ciberseguridad (CISA)

Cybersecurity vaccine: Vacuna de ciberseguridad

Cyberstalking (Internet harassment): Ciberacoso

Cyberterrorism: Ciberterrorismo

Cyberwar (cyberwarfare): Ciberguerra (guerra cibernética)

Cyberweapon: Arma cibernética

Cyclic redundancy check (CRC): Comprobación de redundancia cíclica (CRC)

D

Dark pattern: Patrón oscuro

Dark web: Dark web (web oscura, Internet oscura)

Data: Datos

Data access: Acceso a datos

Data breach: Filtración de datos (vulneración de datos)

Data broker: Broker de datos (vendedor de datos)

Data checker: Comprobación de datos

Data collection: Recopilación de datos

Data crawler: Rastreador de datos

Data encryption: Cifrado de datos

Data hiding: Ocultación de datos

Data infiltration: Infiltración de datos

Data leakage: Fuga de datos (filtración de datos)

Data loss: Pérdida de datos

Data loss prevention (DLP): Prevención de pérdida de datos (DLP)

Data mining: Minería de datos

Data origin: Origen de datos

Data protection delegate (DPD): Delegado/a de protección de datos (DPD)

Data protection impact assessment: Evaluación del impacto sobre la protección de datos (EIPD)

Data security standard (DSS): Estándar de seguridad de datos (DSS)

Data source: Fuente de datos (origen de datos)

Data theft: Robo de datos

Data validation: Validación de datos

Datagram: Datagrama

DCU (Digital Crime Unit): DCU (unidad de crímenes digitales)

DdoS (Distributed Denial of Service): DdoS (denegación de servicio distribuido)

Debugger: Depurador

Debugging: Depuración

Decentralized Exchange (DEX): Plataforma de cambio descentralizada (DEX)

Deceptive: Engañoso/a (falaz)

Decipherment: Descifrado (desciframiento)

Declared data (zero-party data): Datos declarados (zero-party data)

Decoding: Descodificación

Decoy: Señuelo

Decryption (decrypting): Desencriptación (descifrado)

Deep web: Web profunda (Internet profunda)

Deepfake: Falsedad profunda (medios sintéticos)

Defacement: Desfiguración

Defender: Defensor

Demilitarized zone (DMZ): Zona desmilitarizada (DMZ)

Denial of service (DoS): Denegación de servicio (DoS)

Dependability: Confiabilidad (fiabilidad)

Desinformation: Desinformación

Detected: Detectado/a

Detection: Detección

DEX (Decentralized Exchange): DEX (plataforma de cambio descentralizada)

Digital crime unit (DCU): Unidad de crímenes digitales (DCU)

Digital signature: Firma digital

Digital twin (evil twin): Doble digital (gemelo malvado)

Disaster recovery plan (DRP): Plan de recuperación de desastres (PRD)

Disinfection: Desinfección

Dispersion: Dispersión

Distributed denial of service (DdoS): Denegación de servicio distribuido (DdoS)

Distributed denial-of-service attack (DdoS attack): Ataque de denegación de servicio distribuido (ataque DDoS)

DLP (Data Loss Prevention): DLP (prevención de pérdida de datos)

DMZ (DeMilitarized Zone): DMZ (zona desmilitarizada)

Document cracking: Descifrado de documentos

Dolphin: Delfín

Doppelgänger (digital twin, evil twin): Doppelgänger (doble digital, gemelo malvado)

DoS (Denial of Service): DoS (denegación de servicio)

DPD (Data Protection Delegate): DPD (Delegado/a de Protección de Datos)

DPIA (Data Protection Impact Assessment): EIPD (Evaluación del Impacto sobre la Protección de Datos)

Dropper: Dropper (instalador de malware)

DRP (Disaster Recovery Plan): PRD (Plan de Recuperación de Desastres)

DSS (Data Security Standard): DSS (estándar de seguridad de datos)

Dummy: Ficticio/a

Dummy form: Formulario ficticio

Dummy signer: Firmante ficticio

E

EaaS (Exploit as a Service): EaaS (exploit como servicio)

Eavesdropping: Escucha clandestina (interceptación)

EDI (Electronic Data Interchange): EDI (intercambio electrónico de datos)

Electronic mail (e-mail): Correo electrónico (e-mail)

Electronic signature: Firma electrónica

Electronic trust (E-trust): Confianza electrónica

Encapsulation: Encapsulación (encapsulamiento)

Encoder: Codificador

Encrypted: Cifrado/a (encriptado/a)

Encrypted data: Datos cifrados

Encrypted virus: Virus cifrado

Encryption: Cifrado

Encryption algorithm: Algoritmo de cifrado

Encryption key: Clave de cifrado

Encryption setting: Configuración de cifrado

Error correcting code: Código de corrección de errores

Error detecting code: Código de detección de errores

Error detection: Detección de errores

ETH (ether): Ether

Ethereum: Ethereum

Ethical hacker (white hat hacker): Hacker ético/a (hacker de sombrero blanco)

E-trust (electronic trust): Confianza electrónica

Evil twin: Gemelo malvado

Evil twin attack: Ataque Evil Twin (gemelo malvado)

Exchange: Cambio (intercambio, canje)

Executable file (.exe file): Archivo ejecutable (archivo .exe)

Executable file virus: Virus de archivo ejecutable

Executable virus: Virus ejecutable

Exit scam: Estafa de salida

Exploit: Exploit (vulnerabilidad de seguridad)

Exploit as a Service (EaaS): Exploit como servicio (EaaS)

Exploit protection: Protección contra vulnerabilidades

Exposed: Expuesto/a

Exposure: Exposición

Extorsion (blackmail): Extorsión

Extranet: Extranet

F

Face recognition: Reconocimiento facial

Face verification: Verificación facial

Failed attempt (unsuccessful attempt): Intento fallido (intento no satisfactorio, intento incorrecto)

Fake antivirus: Falso antivirus

Fake money: Dinero falso

Fake news: Noticia falsa (noticia engañosa)

False flag: Bandera falsa

False identity: Identidad falsa

False information: Información falsa

False rejection rate (FRR): Tasa de rechazo erróneo (FRR)

Falsification (forgery): Falsificación

Fault: Defecto (error, fallo)

File: Archivo

File exchange: Intercambio de archivos

File name: Nombre de archivo

File name extension: Extensión de nombre de archivo

Fingerprint: Huella dactilar (huella digital)

Fingerprint reader: Lector de huellas digitales

Fingerprint verification: Verificación de huella digital

Firewall: Cortafuegos

Fish (minnow): Pez (pececillo)

Footprint (footprinting): Footprint (buscar datos públicos sobre un sistema)

Forensic: Forense

Forged: Falsificado/a

Forged authorization data: Datos de autorización falsificados

Form (application form): Formulario

Formjacking: Ataque de formulario

Fraud (scam, swindle): Fraude (estafa, timo)

Fraud and abuse: Fraude y abuso

Fraudster (scammer, swindler): Defraudador/a (estafador/a, timador/a)

Fraudulent: Fraudulento/a

Fraudulent data: Datos fraudulentos

Fraudulent message: Mensaje fraudulento

Fraudulent website: Sitio web fraudulento

FRR (False Rejection Rate): FRR (tasa de rechazo erróneo)

Full trust: Plena confianza

Fullz (full information): Fullz (información completa)

G

GAN (Generative Adversarial Network): GAN (red adversaria generativa)

Garbled message: Mensaje confuso

Garbled text: Texto incomprensible (texto codificado)

GDPR (General Data Protection Regulation): RGPD (Reglamento General de Protección de Datos)

Generative adversarial network (GAN): Red adversaria generativa (GAN)

Ghost: Fantasma

Ghost account: Cuenta fantasma

Ghost user: Usuario fantasma

GnuPG (GNU Privacy Guard, GPG): GnuPG (GNU Privacy Guard, GPG)

GRC (Governance, Risk and Compliance): GRC (gobernanza, gestión de riesgos y cumplimiento)

Grey hat hacker: Hacker de sombrero gris

Grooming (child grooming): Grooming (captación de menores)

H

Hack: Hack (truco, manipulación, alteración)

Hackathon (hackfest): Hackathon (hackatón, maratón de hackers)

Hacker: Hacker (pirata informático/a)

Hacking (computer intrusion): Hackeo (pirateo, piratería informática)

Hacking technique: Técnica de hackeo

Hacktivism: Hacktivismo

Hacktivist: Hacktivista

Harassment: Acoso

Harmful: Perjudicial

Harmless: Inofensivo/a

Hash: Hash (función resumen)

Hazard: Peligro (riesgo)

Herpaderping (hacking technique): Herpaderping (técnica de hackeo)

Hidden: Oculto/a

Hidden code: Código oculto

Hiding: Ocultación

Hijacker: Secuestrador

Hijacking: Secuestro

Hoax: Engaño (bulo, información engañosa)

Hoax virus: Virus engañoso (virus fraudulento)

Hole: Agujero

Hollowing: Vaciado

Homomorphism   : Homomorfismo

Honeynet (honey net): Red trampa

Honeypot: Cebo (señuelo, sistema trampa)

Host: Host (anfitrión)

Host cryptogram: Criptograma del host

Hot wallet: Criptomonedero en caliente

Hybrid attack: Ataque híbrido

Hybrid encryption: Cifrado híbrido

I

IAB (Initial Access Broker): IAB (agente de acceso inicial)

ICA (Integrity, Confidentiality and Availability): ICA (integridad, confidencialidad y disponibilidad)

ICO (Initial Coin Offering): OIM (Oferta Inicial de Moneda)

ICS (Industrial Control System): SCI (Sistema de Control Industrial)

ID: ID

Identification: Identificación

Identity fraud: Usurpación de identidad (fraude de ID)

Identity theft: Robo de identidad (suplantación de ID)

IDS (Intrusion Detection System): IDS (sistema de detección de intrusos)

Immunization: Inmunización

Impostor (fake, phony, fraud, liar, slanderer): Impostor

Imposture (fraud): Impostura

Incident: Incidente (incidencia)

Incident detection: Detección de incidentes

Incident response: Respuesta a incidentes

Industrial control system (ICS): Sistema de control industrial (SCI)

Infected: Infectado/a

Infected file: Archivo infectado

Infection: Infección

Inference: Inferencia

Infiltration: Infiltración

Information leak (information leakage): Fuga de información

Information security: Seguridad de la información

Information security management system (ISMS): Sistema de gestión de la seguridad de la información (SGSI)

InfoSec (Information Security): InfoSec (seguridad de la información)

Infostealer: Ladrón de información

Initial access broker (IAB): Agente de acceso inicial (IAB)

Initial coin offering (ICO): Oferta inicial de moneda (OIM)

Insecure: No seguro

Insider (person with privileged information): Infiltrado/a (persona enterada, persona con información privilegiada)

Integrity: Integridad

Integrity checker: Comprobador de la integridad

Integrity, confidentiality and availability (ICA): Integridad, confidencialidad y disponibilidad (ICA)

Interception: Interceptación

Internet harassment (cyberstalking): Acoso por Internet (ciberacoso)

Internet identity (online identity): Identidad en Internet

Intranet: Intranet

Intruder: Intruso/a

Intrusion: Intrusión (intromisión)

Intrusion detection: Detección de intrusos

Intrusion detection system (IDS): Sistema de detección de intrusos (IDS)

Intrusion detector: Detector de intrusos

Intrusion prevention system (IPS): IPS (sistema de prevención de intrusos)

Intrusive: Intrusivo/a (invasivo/a)

Investigation: Investigación

IoC (Indicator of Compromise): IoC (Indicador de Compromiso)

IPS (Intrusion Prevention System): IPS (sistema de prevención de intrusos)

J

Jailbreaking: Jailbreak (desbloqueo)

Joke program: Programa de broma

Junk mail (spam): Correo basura (correo no desado)

K

KDC (Key Distribution Center): KDC (centro de distribución de claves)

Kerberos (computer network authentication protocol): Kerberos (protocolo de autenticación de redes informáticas)

Key: Clave (llave, tecla)

Key authentication: Autenticación de clave

Key chaining: Encadenamiento de clave

Key distribution center (KDC): Centro de distribución de claves (KDC)

Key encryption: Cifrado de claves

Key exchange: Intercambio de claves

Key generation: Generación de claves

Key generator (keygen): Generador de claves (keygen)

Key management: Gestión de claves (administración de claves)

Key phrase (keyphrase): Frase clave

Key recovery: Recuperación de clave

Key search: Búsqueda de clave

Key search attack: Ataque por búsqueda de clave

Keyboard: Teclado

Keylogger (trojan that records keystrokes): Registrador de teclas (troyano que registra pulsaciones de teclas)

Keylogging (keystroke logging, keyboard capturing): Registro de pulsaciones de teclas

Keystroke: Pulsación de tecla

Knapsack problem (KP): Problema de la mochila (KP)

Known-plaintext attack (KPA): Ataque a texto no cifrado conocido (KPA)

KP (Knapsack Problem): KP (problema de la mochila)

L

Label: Etiqueta

Lack of protection: Falta de protección (desprotección)

LAN (local area network): LAN (red de área local)

Lateral movement: Movimiento lateral

Leakage: Fuga

Leakage of information: Fuga de información

Legal notice: Aviso legal

Legitimate: Legítimo/a

Legitimate code: Código legítimo

License (licence): Licencia

License agreement: Acuerdo de licencia (contrato de licencia)

Link: Enlace (vínculo)

Link encryption: Cifrado de enlace

Local area network (LAN): Red de área local (LAN)

Local attack: Ataque local

Local security authority (LSA): Autoridad de seguridad local (LSA)

Local security policy: Política de seguridad local

Locator: Localizador

Lock: Bloqueo

Logic access control: Control de acceso lógico

Logical threat: Amenaza lógica

Login: Login (acceso, conexión, inicio de sesión)

Logon: Inicio de sesión

Logon rights: Derechos de inicio de sesión

Logon script: Script de inicio de sesión

Logon type: Tipo de inicio de sesión

Long-term encryption key: Clave de cifrado de larga duración

LSA (Local Security Authority): LSA (autoridad de seguridad local)

M

M2M (Machine-to-Machine): M2M (máquina a máquina)

MaaS (Malware as a Service): MaaS (malware como servicio)

MAC (Message Authentication Code): MAC (código de autenticación de mensajes)

Machine learning: Aprendizaje automático

Machine-to-Machine (M2M): Máquina a máquina (M2M)

Magnetic card reader: Tarjeta magnética

Magnetic card reader: Lector de tarjetas magnéticas

Mail: Correo

Malicious: Malicioso/a (malintencionado/a)

Malicious code: Código malicioso

Malicious software (malware): Software malicioso (malware)

Malicious user: Usuario malintencionado

Malinformation: Información maliciosa

Malvertising: Publicidad malintencionada

Malware (malicious software): Malware (software malicioso)

Malware as a service (MaaS): Malware como servicio (MaaS)

Malware family: Familia de malware

Malware packages: Paquetes de malware

Malware process: Proceso de malware

Malware scanner: Escáner de malware

Malware variant: Variante de malware

Malwareless: Ataque sin malware

Managed security service provider (MSSP): Proveedor de servicios de seguridad gestionados

Man-in-the-middle (MitM): Intermediario

Masquerade: Farsa (enmascaramiento)

Masquerader: Enmascarador

Masquerading: Suplantación

Massive data: Datos masivos

Message authentication code (MAC): Código de autenticación de mensajes (MAC)

Metastability: Metaestabilidad

MFA (Multi-Factor Authentication): MFA (autenticación multifactor)

MiCA (Markets in Crypto Assets Regulation): MiCA (reglamento de mercados de criptoactivos)

Miner (cryptominer): Minero/a (criptominero/a)

Mining: Minería (minado, minaje)

Misinformation: Desinformación (información errónea)

Misleading: Confuso (engañoso, erróneo)

Misuse: Uso indebido

Misuse detection: Detección de usos indebidos

MitM (Man-in-the-Middle): MitM (Man-in-the-Middle, intermediario)

Monero (open-source cryptocurrency): Monero (criptomoneda de código abierto)

Monoalphabetic: Monoalfabético/a

MSSP (Managed Security Service Provider): MSSP (proveedor de servicios de seguridad gestionados)

Mule (cybermule, money mule): Mula (cibermula)

Multi-factor authentication (MFA): Autenticación multifactor (MFA)

N

NAP (Network Access Protection): NAP (protección de acceso a redes)

Native cryptocurrency : Criptomoneda nativa

Network: Red

Network access protection (NAP): Protección de acceso a redes (NAP)

Network address: Dirección de red

Network device: Dispositivo de red

Network security: Seguridad de red

Network security key: Clave de seguridad de red

Network traffic: Tráfico de red

NFT (Non-Fungible Token): NFT (token no fungible)

NGFW (New Generation FireWall): NGFW (cortafuegos de nueva generación)

Nigerian letter scam: Estafa de las cartas nigerianas

Nigerian scam: Estafa nigeriana (timo nigeriano)

Non-fungible token (NFT): Token no fungible (NFT)

Non-root certificate: Certificado no raíz

Notarization: Notarización

Nuke: Nuke (ataque)

O

Obfuscation: Ofuscación

Oblivious transfer: Transferencia inconsciente

One-Time Password (OTP): Contraseña de un solo uso (OTP)

Online attack: Ataque en línea

Online identity (Internet identity): Identidad en línea (identidad en Internet)

Online piracy: Piratería en línea (piratería informática)

Online scam: Estafa en línea

Online store: Tienda en línea (tienda online, tienda virtual)

Open data: Datos abiertos

Open source: Código abierto (fuente abierta)

Open source intelligence (OSINT): Inteligencia de fuentes abiertas (OSINT)

Open system: Sistema abierto

Open systems interconnection (OSI): Interconexión de sistemas abiertos

Opportunity: Oportunidad

OSINT (Open Source INTelligence): OSINT (inteligencia de fuentes abiertas)

OT (Oblivious transfer): Transferencia inconsciente

OTP (One-Time Password): OTP (contraseña de un solo uso)

Outsider threat: Amenaza externa

Overlay (overlay attack): Overlay (ataque de superposición)

Overwriting virus: Virus de sobreescritura

P

P2P (Peer-to-Peer): P2P (Peer-to-Peer, de igual a igual)

P2P payments: Pagos P2P

P3P (Platform for Privacy Preferences): P3P (plataforma para preferencias de privacidad)

Packet: Paquete

Packet injection: Inyección de paquetes

Packet traffic: Tráfico de paquetes

Parental control: Control parental

Passive attack: Ataque pasivo

Passphrase: Frase de contraseña

Password: Contraseña

Password attack: Ataque de contraseña

Password change: Cambio de contraseña

Password cracker: Descifrador de contraseñas

Password cracking techniques: Técnicas de descifrado de contraseñas

Password manager: Gestor de contraseñas

Password policy: Política de contraseñas

Password spraying: Pulverización de contraseñas

Patch: Parche

PCI DSS (Payment Card Industry Data Security Standard): PCI DSS (estándar de seguridad de datos para la industria de tarjetas de pago)

Peer-to-Peer (P2P): Peer-to-Peer (de igual a igual, P2P)

Penetration: Penetración (intrusión informática)

Penetration testing (pen test): Prueba de penetración (prueba de intrusión)

Perfect Forward Secrecy (PFS): Confidencialidad directa total (PFS)

Personal data: Datos personales

Personal identification number (PIN): Número de identificación personal (PIN)

Personally Identifiable Information (PII): Información de identificación personal (PII)

PFS (Perfect Forward Secrecy): PFS (confidencialidad directa total)

PGP (Pretty Good Privacy): PGP (privacidad bastante buena)

Pharming (malicious code to direct victims to spoofed websites): Pharming (ciberataque donde se manipula el tráfico de un sitio web)

Phisher: Suplantador de identidad

Phishing: Suplantación de identidad

Phishing mail: Correo de suplantación

Phone (telephone): Teléfono

Phone call: Llamada telefónica

Phone tapping: Escucha telefónica (pinchazo telefónico)

Physical threat: Amenaza física

Piggybacking (tailgating): Piggybacking (tailgating)

PII (Personally Identifiable Information): PII (información de identificación personal)

PIN (Personal Identification Number): PIN (número de identificación personal)

Piracy: Piratería

Pixel stuffing: Relleno de píxeles

PKD (Public Key Directory): PKD (directorio de claves públicas)

PKI (Public Key Infrastructure): ICP (Infraestructura de Clave Pública)

Platform for privacy preferences (P3P): Plataforma para preferencias de privacidad (P3P)

PoC (Proof of Concept): PoC (prueba de concepto)

Poisoning: Envenenamiento

Polyalphabetic: Polialfabético/a

Polygram: Poligrama

Polygraphic: Poligráfico/a

Polymorphic: Polimórfico/a

Polymorphism: Polimorfismo

PoS (Proof of Stake): PoS (prueba de participación)

PoW (Proof of Work): PoW (prueba de trabajo)

Pretty good privacy (PGP): Privacidad bastante buena (PGP)

Prevention: Prevención

Privacy: Privacidad

Privacy policy: Política de privacidad

Private blockchain: Cadena de bloques privada

Private key algorithm: Algoritmo de clave privada

Process ghosting (executable image altering attack): Process ghosting (ataque de manipulación de imágenes ejecutables)

Product vulnerability: Vulnerabilidad del producto

Proof: Prueba (comprobación, demostración)

Proof of concept (PoC): Prueba de concepto (PoC)

Proof of stake (PoS): Prueba de participación (PoS)

Proof of work (PoW): Prueba de trabajo (PoW)

Propagation: Propagación

Protection: Protección

Provider: Proveedor

Pseudonymization: Pseudonimización (seudonimización)

Pseudorandom: Pseudoaleatorio/a

Public blockchain: Cadena de bloques pública

Public key algorithm: Algoritmo de clave pública

Public key directory (PKD): Directorio de claves públicas (PKD)

Public key infrastructure (PKI): Infraestructura de clave pública (ICP)

Pyramid scheme: Esquema piramidal (estafa piramidal)

Q

QR code: Código QR

Qrishing (phishing attack through QR codes): Qrishing (ataque de phishing a través de códigos QR)

QS (Quadratic Sieve): QS (criba cuadrática)

Quadruple extorsión: Cuádruple extorsión

Quantum cryptography: Criptografía cuántica

Quarantine: Cuarentena

Quarantined devices: Dispositivos en cuarentena

Quarantined messages: Mensajes en cuarentena

Quarantined threats: Amenazas en cuarentena

R

RaaS (Ransomware as a Service): RaaS (ransomware como servicio)

Random: Aleatorio/a

Random data: Datos aleatorios

Random number: Número aleatorio

Random number generator: Generador de números aleatorios

Ransom: Rescate

Ransomware: Ransomware (malware de rescate, secuestro de datos)

Ransomware as a service (RaaS): Ransomware como servicio (RaaS)

RAT (Remote Access Trojan): RAT (troyano de acceso remoto)

Recognition (reconnaissance): Reconocimiento

Recovery: Recuperación

Recovery key: Clave de recuperación

Red key: Clave roja

Restriction: Restricción

Retrovirus: Retrovirus

Reverse engineering: Ingeniería inversa

RFID (Radio Frequency Identification): RFID (identificación por radiofrecuencia)

Risk: Riesgo

RNG (Random Number Generator): RNG (generador de números aleatorios)

Robot network (botnet): Red de robots (botnet)

Rogue: Deshonesto/a (corrupto/a, fraudulento/a)

Rogueware (malicious software that misleads users into believing there is a virus on their computer): Rogueware (software malicioso que hace creer que hay un virus en el sistema)

Romantic scam: Estafa romántica (fraude romántico)

Root certificate: Certificado raíz

Rooting: Rooting (rooteo)

Rootkit (malicious software): Rootkit (software malicioso)

RSA (Rivest-Shamir-Adleman, public key encryption method): RSA (Rivest, Shamir y Adleman, sistema criptográfico de clave pública)

Rug pull: Tirón de alfombra

S

Sabotage (cybersabotage): Sabotaje (cibersabotaje)

SAC (Strict Avalanche Criterion): SAC (criterio estricto de avalancha)

Sandbox: Entorno de pruebas aislado

SCADA (Supervisory Control and Data Acquisition): SCADA (control de supervisión y adquisición de datos)

Scalability: Escalabilidad

Scam: Estafa (timo, fraude)

Scammer: Estafador/a (timador/a, defraudador/a)

Scareware: Malware para asustar

Search: Búsqueda

Secrecy: Confidencialidad (secreto)

Secret key: Clave secreta

Secret key algorithm: Algoritmo de clave secreta

Secret key encryption: Cifrado de clave secreta

Secret sharing (secret splitting): Compartición de secretos

Secure: Seguro/a

Secure electronic transaction (SET): Transacción electronica segura (SET)

Security (safety): Seguridad

Security descriptor: Descriptor de seguridad

Security master plan (SMP): Plan director de seguridad (PDS)

Security operations center (SOC): Centro de operaciones de seguridad (SOC)

Security policy: Política de seguridad

Security token: Token de seguridad

Security violation: Violación de seguridad

Security zone: Zona de seguridad

Self-healing: Recuperación automática (autorrecuperación)

Self-recovering: Autorrecuperación

Sensitive: Sensible (confidencial)

Sensitive data (confidential data): Datos confidenciales

SET (Secure Electronic Transaction): SET (transacción electronica segura)

Setting: Configuración (ajuste, valor)

Setup: Configuración (instalación, preparación)

Setup time: Tiempo de instalación (tiempo de preparación)

Sexting (sex messaging): Sexting (envío de contenido sexual)

Sextorsion (sexual extorsion): Sextorsión (extorsión sexual)

SFTP (Secure File Transfer Protocol): SFTP (protocolo transferencia segura de archivos)

Shallowfake (cheapfake, fake media produced using easily available and cheap tools): Shallowfake (cheapfake, técnicas básicas de edición de vídeo para crear engaños)

Shoulder surfing: Espionaje por encima del hombro

SIEM (Security Information and Event Management): SIEM (administración de eventos e información de seguridad)

Signature: Firma

Signer: Firmante

SIM swapping (SIM swap fraud): Fraude de la SIM duplicada

Skimmer (device that copies credit cards): Skimmer (dispositivo que copia de tarjetas de crédito)

Skimming (theft of credit and debit card data and PIN numbers): Skimming (fraude a las tarjetas bancarias y números PIN)

Sleeping virus: Virus latente

Smishing (SMS phishing): Smishing (phishing por SMS)

SMP (Security Master Plan): PDS (Plan Director de Seguridad)

SMS phishing (smishing): Phishing por SMS (smishing)

Sniffer: Husmeador (rastreador)

Sniffing: Sniffing (captura de tráfico de red)

SOC (Security Operations Center): SOC (centro de operaciones de seguridad)

Social engineer: Ingeniero/a social

Social engineering: Ingeniería social (piratería social)

Software: Software (programa)

Software attack: Ataque de software (ataque lógico)

Software counterfeiting: Falsificación de software

Software cracking (code cracking): Pirateo de software, descifrado, cracking)

Software piracy: Piratería de software

Software pirate: Pirata informático/a

Software wallet (cryptocurrency wallet based on software): Billetera de software (criptomonedero en línea)

Spam: Spam (correo no deseado, correo basura)

Spammer (person who sends spam): Spammer (emisor/a de correo basura)

Spamming (sending of multiple unsolicited emails or text messages): Spamming (envío masivo de correo basura, inundación)

Speech recognition: Reconocimiento del habla

Spider (crawler): Araña

Spoof: Suplantación (falsificación)

Spoofed: Suplantado/a

Spoofed sender: Remitente suplantado (remitente falsificado)

Spoofed user: Usuario con identidad suplantada

Spoofing: Suplantación de identidad

Spy: Espía

Spyware: Software espía (programa espía)

SSH (Secure Shell) : SSH (shell seguro)

SSID (Service Set Identifier): SSID (identificador de conjunto de servicios)

SSL (Secure Sockets Layer): SSL (capa de sockets seguros)

SSL certificate: Certificado SSL

Stable coin: Moneda estable

Stealer: Ladrón

Stealth: Sigiloso/a (oculto/a, furtivo/a)

Stealth virus: Virus oculto (virus furtivo)

Steganalysis: Esteganálisis

Steganography: Esteganografía

Stolen data: Datos robados

Strong algorithm: Algoritmo fuerte

Strong cryptography: Criptografía sólida

Strong password: Contraseña segura (contraseña robusta)

Successful attempt: Intento satisfactorio (intento correcto)

Superencryption (superencipherment): Supercifrado

Surface web: Web visible

Suspicious: Sospechoso/a

Suspicious e-mail: Correo sospechoso

Suspicious network traffic: Tráfico de red sospechoso

Suspicious pattern detection: Detección de patrones sospechosos

Swap (exchange): Intercambio

Swindle (scam, fraud): Timo (estafa, engaño, fraude)

Swindler (hustler, scammer, diddler): Timador/a (estafador/a)

T

Tag: Etiquea

Tailgating (piggybacking): Tailgating (piggybacking)

Tampered (tampered with): Manipulado/a (alterado/a)

Tampering: Manipulación (alteración)

TAP (Targeted Attack Protection): TAP (protección contra ataques dirigidos)

Test (testing): Prueba (test)

Text bomb (text bombing): Mensaje bomba

Third-party code: Código de terceros

Third-party cookie: Cookie de terceros

Threat: Amenaza

Threat assessment: Evaluación de la amenaza

Threat detection: Detección de amenazas

Threat intelligence: Inteligencia sobre amenazas

Timestamp: Sello de tiempo (marca de tiempo)

To authenticate: Autenticar

To black list: Poner en la lista negra

To blackmail: Chantajear

To check: Comprobar

To click: Hacer clic

To collect: Recopilar (recabar)

To connect: Conectar

To debug: Depurar

To decipher: Descifrar (desencriptar)

To decode: Descodificar

To detect (to spot): Detectar

To download: Bajar (descargar)

To encipher (to encrypt): Cifrar (encriptar)

To encode: Codificar

To erase: Borrar

To expire: Expirar (caducar, vencer)

To extort: Extorsionar

To fix: Corregir (arreglar, solucionar, reparar)

To forward: Reenviar

To get access: Obtener acceso

To hide: Ocultar

To hijack: Secuestrar

To install: Instalar

To interrupt: Interrumpir

To jailbreak (to remove limitations put in place by a device's manufacturer): Liberar (eliminar las limitaciones de un dispositivo impuestas por el fabricante)

To keep track: Realizar el seguimiento

To learn: Aprender

To legitimate: Legitimar

To lock: Bloquear

To log in (to log on, to sign in): Iniciar sesión

To mine (to generate cryptocurrencies): Minar (generar criptomonedas)

To misinform (to misreport): Desinformar (informar mal)

To mislead: Confundir (engañar, falsear)

To modify: Modificar

To nuke: Nukear (realizar un ataque)

To press: Presionar

To query: Consultar

To raise an alert: Generar una alerta

To remove: Quitar (eliminar)

To report: Informar (notificar)

To restart: Reiniciar

To safeguard: Salvaguardar (proteger)

To scam (to swindle): Estafar (timar)

To score: Puntuar

To search: Buscar

To set: Configurar (establecer)

To spoof: Suplantar

To spread: Propagar

To spy: Espiar

To strengthen: Reforzar (fortalecer)

To swap: Intercambiar

To swindle (to scam, to cheat): Timar (estafar, engañar)

To tag: Etiquetar

To transfer: Transferir

To trigger: Desencadenar (activar)

To unsubscribe: Cancelar suscripción (darse de baja de una suscripción)

To update: Actualizar

To upload: Subir (cargar)

To victimize: Victimizar

Token: Token (ficha, criptovalor)

Token cracking: Descifrado de token

Tokenization: Tokenización

TPM (Trusted Platform Module): TPM (módulo de plataforma segura)

Trace: Traza (seguimiento)

Trace flag: Marcador de seguimiento

Trace table: Tabla de seguimiento

Traceability: Trazabilidad

Track (tracking): Pista (seguimiento)

Tracking code: Código de seguimiento

Trademark: Marca comercial

Traffic: Tráfico

Transmission control protocol/internet protocol (TCP/IP): Protocolo de control de transmisión/protocolo de Internet (TCP/IP)

Transparency: Transparencia

Transport layer security (TLS): Seguridad de la capa de transporte (TLS)

Trapdoor: Puerta de captura (trampa)

Tree view: Vista de árbol

Triple extorsión: Triple extorsión

Trojan: Troyano

Trojan dropper: Troyano dropper (troyano cuentagotas)

Trojan horse: Caballo de Troya (troyano)

Trust: Confianza

Trust level: Nivel de confianza

Trust list: Lista de confianza

Trustability: Confiabilidad

Trustable: Confiable (de confianza)

Trustable certificate: Certificado confiable

Trusted computing (TC): Computación confiable (TC)

Trusted root certificate: Certificado raíz de confianza

Trusted third party (TTP): Tercero de confianza (TTP)

Trustworthiness: Confianza (confiabilidad, integridad)

TLS (Transport Layer Security): TLS (seguridad de la capa de transporte)

Two-factor authentication (2FA): Autenticación de dos factores (2FA)

U

Unauthorized: No autorizado/a (sin autorización)

Unauthorized user: Usuario no autorizado

Unavailability: No disponibilidad (indisponibilidad)

Underprotection: Protección insuficiente

Universal serial bus (USB): Bus serie universal (USB)

Unknown sender: Remitente desconocido

Unlawful access: Acceso ilegal

Unsuccessful attempt (failed attempt): Intento no satisfactorio (intento incorrecto, intento fallido)

USB (Universal Serial Bus): USB (bus serie universal)

User: Usuario/a

User account: Cuenta de usuario

User authentication: Autenticación de usuario

User code: Código de usuario

User identification code: Código de identificación de usuario

User interface (UI): Interfaz de usuario (IU, UI)

User name: Nombre de usuario

Utility token: Token de utilidad

V

VA (Validation Authority): VA (autoridad de validación)

Validation: Validación

Validity check: Comprobación de validez

Victim: Víctima

Victim of fraud: Víctima de un fraude

Video surveillance: Videovigilancia (vigilancia por vídeo)

Videoconference bombing (zoombombing): Asalto de videoconferencia (zoombombing)

Violation (infringement, breach): Violación (infracción, vulneración)

Virtual network: Red virtual

Virtual private network (VPN): Red privada virtual (VPN)

Virtual wallet: Monedero virtual

Virtualization: Virtualización

Virus: Virus

Virus detection: Detección de virus

Virus detection software: Software de detección de virus

Virus signature file: Archivo de firmas de virus

Virus variant: Variante de virus

Vishing (voice phishing, VoIP phishing): Vishing (phishing por voz)

Voice assistant (chatbot, talkbot): Asistente de voz (asistente virtual, chatbot)

Voice identification: Identificación de la voz

Voice phishing (vishing): Phishing por voz (vishing)

Voice recognition: Reconocimiento de voz

Volatility: Volatilidad

VPN (Virtual Private Network): VPN (red privada virtual)

Volatility: Volatilidad

Vulnerability: Vulnerabilidad

Vulnerability analysis: Análisis de vulnerabilidades

Vulnerability scanner: Escáner de vulnerabilidades

W

Wallet: Monedero (billetera, cartera)

War game: Juego de guerra

Watering hole attack: Ataque de abrevadero

Weak password: Contraseña débil (contraseña no segura)

WEP (Wired Equivalent Privacy): WEP (privacidad equivalente a cableado)

Whale: Ballena

Whaling attack (whaling phishing): Caza de ballenas (fraude del CEO)

White hat (white hat hacker, ethical hacker): Hacker de sombrero blanco (hacker ético/a, hacker bueno/a)

Windowing: Ventanización

Wired equivalent privacy (WEP): Privacidad equivalente a cableado (WEP)

Wireless (cordless): Inalámbrico/a (sin hilos)

Wireless wide area network: Red de área extensa inalámbrica

Wiretapper: Persona que pincha teléfonos

Wiretapping: Intervención telefónica (pinchazo telefónico)

Wizard: Asistente

Word extraction dictionary: Diccionario de extracción de palabras

Worm: Gusano

WWW (World Wide Web): WWW (telaraña mundial)

X

XMR (monero, open-source cryptocurrency): XMR (monero, criptomoneda de código abierto)

XSS (Cross Site Scripting): XSS (scripting entre sitios)

XSS attack: Ataque de XSS (ataque de scripts de sitios)

Z

Zero trust: Confianza cero

Zero-click attack (zero-click hack): Ataque de clic cero

Zero-day (0-day): Día cero (vulnerabilidad de día cero)

Zero-day attack: Ataque de día cero

Zero-day URL: Dirección URL de día cero

Zero-party data (declared data): Zero-party data (datos declarados)

ZKP (Zero Knowledge Proof): ZKP (prueba de conocimiento nulo)

Zombie (device infected with malware that is controlled by a hacker): Zombi (dispositivo infectado por malware y que está controlado por un hacker)

Zoombombing (videoconference bombing): Zoombombing (asalto de videoconferencia)

PARTE II: ESPAÑOL-INGLÉS

A

AaaS (acceso como servicio): AaaS (Access as a Service)

Abuso: Abuse

Acceso: Access

Acceso a datos: Data access

Acceso ilegal: Unlawful access

Acoso: Harassment

Acoso por Internet (ciberacoso): Internet harassment (cyberstalking)

Actualizar: To update (to upgrade)

Administración de claves (gestión de claves): Key management

Adversario: Adversary

Adware (software que muestra anuncios): Adware

AES (estándar de cifrado avanzado): AES (Advanced Encryption Standard)

Agencia de seguridad de infraestructura y ciberseguridad (CISA): Cybersecurity and Infrastructure Security Agency (CISA)

Agente de acceso inicial (IAB): Initial access broker (IAB)

Agente de seguridad de acceso a la nube (CASB): Cloud access security broker (CASB)

Agujero: Hole

Ajuste (sintonización): Tuning

Aleatorio/a: Random

Alerta: Alert

Algoritmo: Algorithm

Algoritmo criptográfico: Cryptographic algorithm

Algoritmo de caja negra: Black box algorithm

Algoritmo de cifrado: Encryption algorithm

Algoritmo de clave privada: Private key algorithm

Algoritmo de clave pública: Public key algorithm

Algoritmo de clave secreta: Secret key algorithm

Algoritmo fuerte: Strong algorithm

Altcoin (criptomoneda alternativa): Altcoin (alternative coin)

Amenaza: Threat

Amenaza externa: Outsider threat

Amenaza física: Physical threat

Amenaza persistente avanzada (APT): Advanced persistent threat (APT)

Amenazas en cuarentena: Quarantined threats

Análisis de vulnerabilidades: Vulnerability analysis

Anomalía: Anomaly

Anonimato: Anonymity

Anonimización: Anonymization (anonymisation)

Anónimo/a: Anonymous

Antimalware (software antimalicioso): Antimalware

Antispam (protección contra correo no deseado): Antispam

Antispyware (software antiespía): Antispyware

Antisuplantación: Antispoofing

Antivirus: Antivirus

Anzuelo: Bait

Apagón: Blackout

Aplicación en la nube: Cloud app

Aplicación nativa en la nube: Cloud native app

Aprender: To learn

Aprendizaje automático: Machine learning

Araña: Spider (crawler)

Archivo: File

Archivo adjunto (datos adjuntos): Attachment

Archivo de firmas de virus: Virus signature file

Archivo ejecutable (archivo .exe): Executable file (.exe file)

Archivo infectado: Infected file

Arma cibernética: Cyberweapon

Asalto de videoconferencia (zoombombing): Videoconference bombing (zoombombing)

Asistente de voz (chatbot): Voice assistant (chatbot, talkbot)

ASR (reducción de la superficie de ataque): ASR (Attack Surface Reduction)

Atacante: Attacker

Ataque: Attack (assault)

Ataque a texto no cifrado conocido (KPA): Known-plaintext attack (KPA)

Ataque activo: Active attack

Ataque BlackNurse: BlackNurse attack

Ataque de abrevadero: Watering hole attack

Ataque de clic cero: Zero-click attack (zero-click hack)

Ataque de contraseña: Password attack

Ataque de denegación de servicio distribuido (ataque DDoS): Distributed denial-of-service attack (DdoS attack)

Ataque de día cero: Zero-day attack

Ataque de formulario: Formjacking

Ataque de software: Software attack

Ataque de superposición: Overlay attack

Ataque de XSS (ataque de scripts de sitios): XSS attack

Ataque en línea: Online attack

Ataque Evil Twin (gemelo malvado): Evil twin attack

Ataque local: Local attack

Ataque pasivo: Passive attack

Ataque personalizado: Customized attack

Ataque por búsqueda de clave: Key search attack

Ataque por fuerza bruta: Brute force attack

Ataque sin malware: Malwareless

Autenticación (autentificación): Authentication

Autenticación de clave: Key authentication

Autenticación de dos factores (2FA): Two-factor authentication (2FA)

Autenticación de usuario: User authentication

Autenticación multifactor (MFA): Multi-factor authentication (MFA)

Autenticar: To authenticate

Autenticidad: Authenticity

Autoencriptación: Autocryptography

Automorfismo: Automorphism

Autoridad: Authority

Autoridad de autenticación: Authentication authority

Autoridad certificadora (CA): Certification Authority (CA)

Autoridad de seguridad local (LSA): Local security authority (LSA)

Autoridad de validación (VA): Validation authority (VA)

Autorización: Authorization

Autorrecuperación: Self-recovering (self-healing)

Avalancha: Avalanche

Aviso legal: Legal notice

B

B2B (negocio a negocio): B2B (Business to Business)

B2C (negocio a consumidor): B2C (Business to Consumer)

BaaS (cadena de bloques como servicio): BaaS (Blockchain as a Service)

Bajada (descarga): Download

Bajar (descargar): To download

Bandera falsa: False flag

Bastión: Bastion

BEC (compromiso de correo electrónico empresarial): BEC (Business Email Compromise)

BIA (análisis de impacto de negocio): BIA (Business Impact Analysis)

Billetera de software (criptomonedero en línea): Software wallet (cryptocurrency wallet based on software)

Bitcoin: Bitcoin

Bloqueo: Lock

Bluebugging (forma de ataque Bluetooth): Bluebugging

Bluejacking (envío de mensajes con Bluetooth): Bluejacking

Bluesnarfing (ataque a través de Bluetooth): Bluesnarfing

Bombardeo: Bombing

Borrar: To erase

Bot (robot): Bot (robot, software robot)

Botnet (red de robots): Botnet (robot network)

Bus serie universal (USB): Universal serial bus (USB)

Buscar: To search

Búsqueda de clave: Key search

C

CA (autoridad certificadora): CA (Certification Authority)

CaaS (cibercrimen como servicio): CaaS (Cybercrime as a Service)

Caballo de Troya (troyano): Trojan horse (trojan)

Cadena de bloques: Blockchain

Cadena de bloques privada: Private blockchain

Cadena de bloques pública: Public blockchain

Cambio de contraseña: Password change

Cancelar suscripción: To unsubscribe

CAPEC (enumeración y clasificación de patrones de ataque comunes): CAPEC (Common Attack Pattern Enumeration and Classification)

Captación de menores (grooming): Child grooming

CAPTCHA (test público y completamente automatizado de Turing para diferenciar computadoras de humanos): CAPTCHA (Completely Automated Public Turing test to tell Computers and Humans Apart)

Captura de tráfico de red: Sniffing

Carding (estafa de las tarjetas bancarias): Carding

CASB (agente de seguridad de acceso a la nube): CASB (Cloud Access Security Broker)

Catfishing (catphishing, impostura): Catfishing (catphishing)

CAVP (programa de validación de algoritmos criptográficos): CAVP (Cryptographic Algorithm Validation Program)

Caza de ballenas (fraude del CEO): Whaling attack (whaling phishing)

CDO (director/a de datos, DD): CDO (Chief Data Officer)

Cebo (señuelo, sistema trampa): Bait (honeypot)

Cebo de clics (ciberanzuelo): Clickbait

Centro de distribución de claves (KDC): Key distribution center (KDC)

Centro de operaciones de seguridad (SOC): Security operations center (SOC)

CERT (equipo de respuesta ante emergencias informáticas): CERT (Computer Emergency Response Team)

Certificado: Certificate

Certificado ciego: Blind certificate

Certificado confiable: Trustable certificate

Certificado de autenticidad (COA): Certificate of authenticity (COA)

Certificado no raíz: Non-root certificate

Certificado raíz: Root certificate

Certificado raíz de confianza: Trusted root certificate

Certificado SSL: SSL certificate

Chantaje: Blackmail

Chantajear: To blackmail

Chatbot (asistente de voz, asistente virtual): Chatbot (talkbot, voice assistant)

Ciberacoso: Cyberstalking (Internet harassment)

Ciberactivismo: Cyberactivism (Internet activism)

Ciberanalista: Cyberanalist

Ciberanzuelo (cebo de clics): Clickbait

Ciberataque: Cyberattack

Cibercafé: Cybercafé (Internet café)

Cibercrimen (ciberdelito, ciberdelincuencia): Cybercrime

Cibercrimen como servicio (CaaS): Cybercrime as a Service (CaaS)

Cibercultura: Cyberculture

Ciberdelincuencia (cibercrimen, ciberdelito): Cybercrime

Ciberdelincuente: Cybercriminal

Ciberderecho: Cyber law

Ciberejercicio: Cyberexercice

Ciberespionaje: Cyber-espionage (cyberspying)

Ciberestafa (estafa en línea): Cyberscam (online scam)

Ciberguerra (guerra cibernética): Cyberwar (cyberwarfare)

Cibermula: Cybermule (money mule)

Cibernauta: Cybernaut

Cibernética: Cybernetics

Cibersabotaje: Cybersabotage

Ciberseguridad: Cybersecurity

Ciberterrorismo: Cyberterrorism

Cibersabotaje: Cybersabotage

Cifrado: Encryption

Cifrado de claves: Key encryption

Cifrado de datos: Data encryption

Cifrado híbrido: Hybrid encryption

Cifrado/a (encriptado/a): Encrypted

Cifrar (encriptar): To cipher (to cypher, to encipher, to encrypt)

CISA (agencia de seguridad de infraestructura y ciberseguridad): CISA (Cybersecurity and Infrastructure Security Agency)

Clasificado/a (reservado/a): Classified

Clave de cifrado: Encryption key

Clave de cifrado de larga duración: Long-term encryption key

Clave de recuperación: Recovery key

Clave secreta: Secret key

Clave de seguridad de red: Network security key

Clave roja: Red key

Clickbait (ciberanzuelo, cebo de clics): Clickbait

Clickjacking (secuestro de clics): Clickjacking

Cloudjacking (cryptojacking en la nube): Cloudjacking

COA (certificado de autenticidad): COA (Certificate Of Authenticity)

Codificador: Encoder

Codificar: To encode

Código: Code

Código de acceso: Access code

Código de autenticación de mensajes (MAC): Message authentication code (MAC)

Código de corrección de errores: Error correcting code

Código de detección de errores: Error detecting code

Código de identificación de usuario: User identification code

Código de seguimiento: Tracking code

Código de terceros: Third-party code

Código de usuario: User code

Código legítimo: Legitimate code

Código malicioso: Malicious code

Código oculto: Hidden code

Código QR: QR code

Combinatoria: Combinatorics

Compartición de secretos: Secret sharing (secret splitting)

Comprobación: Check (checking, verification)

Comprobación de datos: Data check

Comprobación de integridad: Integrity check

Comprobación de redundancia cíclica (CRC): Cyclic redundancy check (CRC)

Comprobación de validez: Validity check

Comprobador: Checker

Comprobador de la integridad: Integrity checker

Comprobar: To check (to verify, to test)

Comprometido/a: Compromised

Compromiso: Compromise

Computador/a (ordenador, equipo): Computer

Computación confiable (TC): Trusted computing (TC)

Computación en la nube (informática en la nube): Cloud computing

Conectar: To connect

Confiabilidad: Trustability

Confiable (de confianza): Trustable

Confianza: Trust

Confianza electrónica: E-trust (electronic trust)

Confidencial: Confidential

Confidencialidad: Confidentiality (secrecy)

Confidencialidad directa total (PFS): Perfect Forward Secrecy (PFS)

Configuración: Configuration (settings, setup)

Configuración de cifrado: Encryption setting

Configurar (establecer): To configure (to set)

Confinamiento: Confinement

Confundir (engañar, falsear): To mislead

Confuso (engañoso, erróneo): Misleading

Consentimiento: Consent

Consultar: To query

Contrafirma: Counter-signature

Contraseña: Password

Contraseña de un solo uso (OTP): One-Time Password (OTP)

Contraseña débil (contraseña no segura): Weak password

Contraseña robusta (contraseña segura): Strong password

Control de acceso: Access control

Control de acceso lógico: Logical access control

Control parental: Parental control

Cookie de terceros: Third-party cookie

Copia de seguridad (copia de respaldo): Backup (backup copy)

Corregir (arreglar, solucionar, reparar): To fix

Correo: Mail

Correo basura (correo no desado): Junk mail (spam)

Correo de suplantación: Phishing mail

Correo electrónico (e-mail): Electronic mail (e-mail)

Correo masivo: Bulk e-mail

Correo no deseado: Spam

Correo sospechoso: Suspicious e-mail

Cortafuegos: Firewall

Cortafuegos de nueva generación (NGFW): New Generation FireWall (NGFW)

CPS (declaración de prácticas de certificación): CPS (Certification Practice Statement)

Cracking (pirateo de software, descifrado): Cracking (software cracking, code cracking)

CRC (comprobación de redundancia cíclica): CRC (Cyclic Redundancy Check)

Credencial: Credential

Criptoactivos: Cryptoassets

Criptoanálisis: Cryptanalysis

Criptoanalista: Cryptanalyst

Criptografía: Cryptography

Criptografía cuántica: Quantum cryptography

Criptografía sólida: Strong cryptography

Criptógrafo/a: Cryptographer

Criptograma: Cryptogram

Criptograma del host: Host cryptogram

Criptología: Cryptology

Criptólogo/a: Cryptologist

Criptominería (minería de criptomonedas): Cryptomining (cryptocurrency mining)

Criptominero/a: Cryptominer

Criptomoneda (moneda criptográfica): Cryptocurrency

Criptomoneda nativa: Native cryptocurrency

Criptomonedero: Cryptowallet

Criptomonedero en caliente: Hot wallet

Criptosistema (sistema criptográfico): Cryptosystem (cryptograhic system)

Criptovirología: Cryptovirology

Criptovirus: Cryptovirus

Criticidad: Criticality

Cryptojacking (criptosecuestro): Cryptojacking

CSIRT (equipo de respuesta ante incidencias de seguridad informática): CSIRT (Computer Security Incidence Response Team)

CSPM (gestión de la postura de seguridad en la nube): CSPM (Cloud Security Posture Management)

CSRF (falsificación de solicitud entre sitios): CSRF (Cross Site Request Forgery)

CTI (inteligencia sobre ciberamenazas): CTI (Cyber Threat Intelligence)

Cuádruple extorsión: Quadruple extorsion

Cuarentena: Quarantine

Cuenta: Account

Cuenta bancaria: Bank account

Cuenta de usuario: User account

Cuenta fantasma: Ghost account

CVE (vulnerabilidades y exposiciones comunes): CVE (Common Vulnerabilities and Exposures)

CVS (puntuación vulnerabilidades comunes): CVS (Common Vulnerability Scoring)

CVSS (sistema de puntuación de vulnerabilidades comunes): CVSS (Common Vulnerability Scoring System)

CWE (enumeración de debilidades comunes): CWE (Common Weaknesses Enumeration)

D

Dark web (web oscura, Internet oscura): Dark web

Darse de baja de una suscripción: To unsubscribe

Datagrama: Datagram

Datos: Data

Datos abiertos: Open data

Datos aleatorios: Random data

Datos cifrados: Encrypted data

Datos confidenciales: Confidential data (sensitive data)

Datos de autorización: Authorization data

Datos de autorización falsificados: Forged authorization data

Datos declarados (zero-party data): Declared data (zero-party data)

Datos fraudulentos: Fraudulent data

Datos masivos: Massive data

Datos personales: Personal data

Datos robados: Stolen data

DCU (unidad de crímenes digitales): DCU (Digital Crime Unit)

DD (director/a de datos): CDO (Chief Data Officer)

DdoS (denegación de servicio distribuido): DdoS (Distributed Denial of Service)

Deep web (web profunda, Internet profunda): Deep web

Deepfake (falsedad profunda, medios sintéticos): Deepfake

Defacement (desfiguración): Defacement

Defecto (error, fallo): Defect (fault)

Defensor: Defender

Defraudador/a (estafador/a, timador/a): Fraudster (scammer, swindler)

Delfín: Dolphin

Delegado/a de protección de datos (DPD): DPD (Data Protection Delegate)

Delito cibernético (cibercrimen, ciberdelito): Cybercrime

Denegación de servicio (DoS): Denial of service (DoS)

Denegación de servicio distribuido (DdoS): Distributed denial of service (DdoS)

Depuración: Debugging

Depurador: Debugger

Depurar: To debug

Descifrado (desencriptación): Decryption (cracking)

Descifrado de contraseñas: Password cracking

Descifrado de documentos: Document cracking

Descifrador de contraseñas: Password cracker

Descifrar: To crack (to decipher)

Descifrar contraseñas: To crack passwords

Descodificación: Decoding

Descodificar: To decode

Descriptor de seguridad: Security descriptor

Desencadenar (activar): To trigger

Desencriptación (descifrado): Decryption (decrypting)

Desfiguración: Defacement

Deshonesto/a (corrupto/a, fraudulento/a): Rogue

Desinfección: Disinfection

Desinformación (información errónea): Misinformation

Desinformar (informar mal): To misinform (to misreport)

Detección: Detection

Detección de amenazas: Threat detection

Detección de errores: Error detection

Detección de incidentes: Incident detection

Detección de intrusos: Intrusion detection

Detección de la firma de ataque: Attack signature detection

Detección de patrones sospechosos: Suspicious pattern detection

Detección de usos indebidos: Misuse detection

Detección de virus: Virus detection

Detectado/a: Detected

Detectar: To detect (to spot)

Detector de intrusos: Intrusion detector

Detector de vulnerabilidades: Vulnerability detector

DEX (plataforma de cambio descentralizada): DEX (Decentralized Exchange)

Día cero (vulnerabilidad de día cero): Zero-day (O-day)

Diccionario de extracción de palabras: Word extraction dictionary

Dinero falsificado (dinero falso): Counterfeit money (fake money)

Dirección de red: Network address

Dirección URL de día cero: Zero-day URL

Director/a de datos (DD): Chief data officer (CDO)

Dispersión: Dispersion

Dispositivo: Device

Dispositivo de red: Network device

Dispositivos en cuarentena: Quarantined devices

DLP (prevención de pérdida de datos): DLP (Data Loss Prevention)

DMZ (zona desmilitarizada): DMZ (DeMilitarized Zone)

Doppelgänger (doble digital, gemelo malvado): Doppelgänger (digital twin, evil twin)

DoS (denegación de servicio): DoS (Denial of Service)

DPD (Delegado/a de Protección de Datos): DPD (Data Protection Delegate)

Dropper (instalador de malware): Dropper

DSS (estándar de seguridad de datos): DSS (Data Security Standard)

E

EaaS (exploit como servicio): EaaS (Exploit as a Service)

EDI (intercambio electrónico de datos): EDI (Electronic Data Interchange

EIPD (Evaluación del Impacto sobre la Protección de Datos): DPIA (Data Protection Impact Assessment)

Encadenamiento de bloques: Block chaining

Encadenamiento de bloques de cifrado: Cipher block chaining (CBC)

Encadenamiento de clave: Key chaining

Encapsulación (encapsulamiento): Encapsulation

Encriptar (cifrar, codificar): To encrypt (to encipher, to encode)

Engaño (bulo, información engañosa): Hoax

Engañoso/a (falaz): Deceptive

Enmascarador: Masquerader

Entorno de pruebas aislado: Sandbox

Envío masivo de correo basura (spamming, inundación): Sending of multiple unsolicited emails or text messages (spamming)

Equipo de respuesta ante incidencias de seguridad informática (CSIRT): Computer security incidence response team (CSIRT)

Escalabilidad: Scalability

Escáner de malware: Malware scanner

Escáner de vulnerabilidades: Vulnerability scanner

Escucha clandestina (interceptación): Eavesdropping

Escucha telefónica: Phone tapping

Espía: Spy

Espiar: To spy

Espionaje por encima del hombro: Shoulder surfing

Esquema piramidal (estafa piramidal): Pyramid scheme

Estafa (timo, fraude): Scam (swindle, fraud)

Estafa bancaria: Bank fraud

Estafa de salida: Exit scam

Estafa del CEO (fraude del CEO, fraude del director ejecutivo): CEO scam (CEO fraud, Chief Executive Officer fraud)

Estafa de las cartas nigerianas: Nigerian letter scam

Estafa nigeriana (timo nigeriano): Nigerian scam

Estafa de las tarjetas bancarias: Carding

Estafa en línea: Online scam

Estafa piramidal (esquema piramidal): Pyramid scheme

Estafa romántica (fraude romántico): Romantic scam

Estafador/a (timador/a, defraudador/a): Scammer (swindler, hustler, diddler, fraudster)

Estafar (timar): **To scam (to swindle)**

Estándar de seguridad de datos (DSS): Data security standard (DSS)

Esteganálisis: Steganalysis

Esteganografía: Steganography

Ether: ETH (ether)

Ethereum: Ethereum

Etiqueta: Label (tag)

Etiquetar: To label (to tag)

Evaluación de la amenaza: Threat assessment

Evaluación de riesgos: Risk assessment

Evaluación de vulnerabilidades: Vulnerability assessment

Evento de riesgo: Risk event

Evaluación del Impacto sobre la Protección de Datos (EIPD): Data Protection Impact Assessment (DPIA)

Evitación (elusión): Avoidance

Expirar (caducar, vencer): To expire

Exploit (vulnerabilidad de seguridad): Exploit

Exploit como servicio (EaaS): Exploit as a Service (EaaS)

Exposición: Exposure

Expuesto/a: Exposed

Extensión de nombre de archivo: File name extension

Extorsión: Extorsion (blackmail)

Extorsión sexual (sextorsión): Sexual extorsion (sextorsion)

Extorsionar: To extort

Extranet: Extranet

F

Falsedad profunda (medios sintéticos): Deepfake

Falsificación: Falsification (forgery, counterfeit)

Falsificación de software: Software counterfeiting

Falsificación de solicitud entre sitios (CSRF): Cross site request forgery (CSRF)

Falsificado/a: Forged

Familia de malware: Malware family

Fantasma: Ghost

Farsa (enmascaramiento): Masquerade

Ficticio/a: Dummy

Filtración (revelación): Filtering (leak)

Filtración de datos: Data leakage (data breach)

Firma: Signature

Firma ciega: Blind signature

Firma del ataque: Attack signatura

Firma digital: Digital signature

Firma electrónica: Electronic signature

Firmante Signer (signatory)

Firmante ficticio: Dummy signer

Footprint (buscar datos públicos sobre un sistema) Footprint (footprinting)

Forense Forensic

Formulario: Form

Formulario ficticio: Dummy form

Frase clave: Key phrase (keyphrase)

Frase de contraseña: Passphrase

Fraude (estafa, timo): Fraud (scam, swindle)

Fraude de la SIM duplicada: SIM swapping (SIM swap fraud)

Fraude del clic: Click fraud

Fraude del director ejecutivo (fraude del CEO, estafa del CEO): Chief Executive Officer fraud (CEO fraud, CEO scam)

Fraude publicitario: Ad fraud (advertising fraud)

Fraude romántico (estafa romántica): Romantic scam

Fraude y abuso: Fraud and abuse

Fraudulento/a: Fraudulent

FRR (tasa de rechazo erróneo): FRR (False Rejection Rate)

Fuerza bruta: Brute force

Fuga: Leakage

Fuga de datos: Data leakage

Fuga de información: Information leakage

Fullz (información completa): Fullz (full information)

G

GAN (red adversaria generativa): GAN (Generative Adversarial Network)

Gemelo malvado: Evil twin

Generador de claves (keygen): Key generator (keygen)

Generador de números aleatorios: Random number generator (RNG)

Generar criptomonedas: To generate cryptocurrencies

Generar una alerta: To raise an alert

Gestión de claves (administración de claves): Key management

Gestión de la postura de seguridad en la nube (CSPM): Cloud security posture management (CSPM)

Gestor de contraseñas: Pasword manager

GPG (GNU Privacy Guard, GnuGPG): GPG (GNU Privacy Guard, GnuGPG)

Grabación de llamada: Call recording

GRC (gobernanza, gestión de riesgos y cumplimiento): GRC (Governance, Risk and Compliance)

Grieta : Crack

Grooming (captación de menores): Grooming (child grooming)

Guerra cibernética (ciberguerra): Cyberwar (cyberwarfare)

Gusano: Worm

Gusano autoejecutable: Autorun worm

Gusano de Internet: Internet worm

H

Hacer clic: To click

Hack (truco, manipulación, alteración): Hack

Hackathon (hackatón, maratón de hackers): Hackathon (hackfest)

Hackeo (pirateo, piratería informática): Hacking (computer intrusion)

Hacker (pirata informático/a): Hacker

Hacker de sombrero azul: Blue hat hacker

Hacker de sombrero blanco (hacker ético/a, hacker bueno/a): White hat hacker (ethical hacker)

Hacker de sombrero gris: Grey hat hacker

Hacker de sombrero negro (pirata, cracker): Black hat hacker (malicious hacker, cracker)

Hacker ético/a (hacker de sombrero blanco): Ethical hacker (white hat hacker)

Hacktivismo: Hacktivism

Hacktivista: Hacktivist

Hash (función resumen): Hash

Herpaderping (técnica de hackeo): Herpaderping (hacking technique)

Homomorfismo: Homomorphism

Honeypot (cebo, señuelo, sistema trampa): Honeypot

Host (anfitrión): Host

Huella dactilar (huella digital): Fingerprint

Husmeador (rastreador): Sniffer

I

IAB (agente de acceso inicial): IAB (Initial Access Broker)

ICA (integridad, confidencialidad y disponibilidad): ICA (Integrity, Confidentiality and Availability)

ICP (Infraestructura de Clave Pública): PKI (Public Key Infrastructure)

ID: ID

Identidad en Internet (identidad en línea): Internet identity (online identity)

Identidad falsa: False identity

Identificación: Identification

IDS (sistema de detección de intrusos): IDS (Intrusion Detection System)

Impostor: Impostor (fake, phony, fraud, liar, slanderer)

Impostura: Imposture (fraud)

Inalámbrico/a (sin hilos): Wireless (cordless)

Incidente (incidencia): Incident (event)

Infección: Infection

Infectado/a: Infected

Inferencia: Inference

Infiltración: Infiltration

Infiltración de datos: Data infiltration

Infiltrado/a (persona con información privilegiada): Insider (person with privileged information)

Información de identificación personal (PII): Personally Identifiable Information (PII)

Información falsa: False information

Información maliciosa: Malinformation

Informar (notificar): To report

InfoSec (seguridad de la información): InfoSec (Information Security)

Infracción: Violation (infringement)

Infraestructura de clave pública (ICP): Public key infrastructure (PKI)

Infringir: To violate

Ingeniería inversa: Reverse engineering

Ingeniería social (piratería social): Social engineering

Ingeniero/a social: Social engineer

Iniciar sesión: To log in (to log on, to sign in)

Inicio de sesión: Login (logon, sign in)

Inmunización: Immunization

Inofensivo/a: Harmless

Insider (infiltrado/a, persona con información privilegiada): Insider (person with privileged information)

Instalador de malware: Dropper

Instalar: To install

Integridad: Integrity

Integridad, confidencialidad y disponibilidad (ICA): Integrity, confidentiality and availability (ICA)

Inteligencia de fuentes abiertas (OSINT): Open source intelligence (OSINT)

Inteligencia sobre ciberamenazas (CTI): Cyber threat intelligence (CTI)

Intento de acceso: Access attempt

Intento no satisfactorio (intento incorrecto, intento fallido): Unsuccessful attempt (failed attempt)

Intento satisfactorio (intento correcto): Successful attempt

Intercambiar: To swap (to exchange)

Intercambio: Swap (exchange)

Intercambio de archivos: File exchange

Intercambio de claves: Key exchange

Intercambio electrónico de datos (EDI): Electronic data interchange (EDI

Interceptación: Interception

Interconexión de sistemas abiertos (OSI): Open systems interconnection (OSI)

Intermediario: Man-in-the-middle (MitM)

Interrumpir: To interrupt

Intervención telefónica (pinchazo telefónico): Wiretapping

Intranet: Intranet

Intrusión: Intrusion

Intrusivo/a (invasivo/a): Intrusive

Intruso/a: Intruder

Investigación: Investigation

IoC (Indicador de Compromiso): IoC (Indicator of Compromise)

IPS (sistema de prevención de intrusos): IPS (Intrusion Prevention System)

J

Jailbreak (desbloqueo): Jailbreaking

Juego de caracteres: Character set

Juego de guerra: War game

K

KDC (centro de distribución de claves): KDC (Key Distribution Center)

Kerberos (protocolo de autenticación de redes informáticas): Kerberos (computer network authentication protocol)

Keygen (generador de claves): Keygen (key generator, key maker)

Keylogger (troyano que registra pulsaciones de teclas, registrador de teclas): Keylogger (trojan that records keystrokes)

KP (problema de la mochila): KP (Knapsack Problem)

KPA (ataque a texto no cifrado conocido): KPA (Known-Plaintext Attack)

L

Ladrón: Stealer

Ladrón de información: Infostealer

LAN (red de área local): LAN (local area network)

Lector de huellas digitales: Fingerprint reader

Lector de tarjetas magnéticas: Magnetic card reader

Legitimar: To legitimate

Legítimo/a: Legitimate

Liberar (eliminar las limitaciones de un dispositivo impuestas por el fabricante): To jailbreak (to remove limitations put in place by a device's manufacturer)

Licencia: License (licence)

Lista de comprobación: Checklist

Lista de confianza: Trust list

Lista negra (lista de bloqueados): Black list

Llamada telefónica: Phone call

Llave: Key

Localizador: Locator

LOPDGDD (Organic Law on Protection of Personal Data and Guarantee of Digital Rights): LOPDGDD (Ley Orgánica de Protección de Datos Personales y Garantía de los Derechos Digitales)

LSA (autoridad de seguridad local): LSA (Local Security Authority)

M

M2M (máquina a máquina): M2M (Machine-to-Machine)

MaaS (malware como servicio): MaaS (Malware as a Service)

MAC (código de autenticación de mensajes)   : MAC (Message Authentication Code)

MFA (autenticación multifactor): MFA (Multi-Factor Authentication)

Malicioso/a (malintencionado/a): Malicious

Malvertising (publicidad malintencionada): Malvertising

Malware (software malicioso): Malware (malicious software)

Malware como servicio (MaaS): Malware as a service (MaaS)

Malware para asustar: Scareware

Manipulación (alteración): Tampering

Manipulado/a (alterado/a): Tampered (tampered with)

Marca comercial: Trademark

Marcador de seguimiento: Trace flag

Máquina a máquina (M2M): Machine-to-Machine (M2M)

Medios sintéticos (falsedad profunda): Deepfake

Mensaje bomba: Text bomb (text bombing)

Mensaje confuso: Garbled message

Mensaje fraudulento: Fraudulent message

Mensajes en cuarentena: Quarantined messages

Mercado negro: Black market

Metaestabilidad: Metastability

MiCA (reglamento de mercados de criptoactivos): MiCA (Markets in Crypto Assets Regulation)

Minar (generar criptomonedas): To mine (to generate cryptocurrencies)

Minería (minado, minaje): Mining

Minería de criptomonedas (criptominería): Cryptocurrency mining (cryptomining)

Minería de datos: Data mining

Minero/a (criptominero/a): Miner (cryptominer)

MitM (Man-in-the-Middle, intermediario): MitM (Man-in-the-Middle)

Modificar: To modify

Módulo de plataforma segura (TPM): Trusted platform module (TPM)

Moneda: Currency (coin)

Moneda criptográfica (criptomoneda): Cryptocurrency

Moneda digital: Digital currency

Moneda falsa (dinero falsificado, dinero falso): Counterfeit money (fake money)

Monedero (billetera, cartera): Wallet

Monedero virtual: Virtual wallet

Monero (criptomoneda de código abierto): Monero (open-source cryptocurrency)

Monoalfabético/a: Monoalphabetic

Movimiento lateral: Lateral movement

MSSP (proveedor de servicios de seguridad gestionados): MSSP (Managed Security Service Provider)

Mula (cibermula): Mule (cybermule, money mule)

N

NAP (protección de acceso a redes): NAP (Network Access Protection)

NFT (token no fungible): NFT (Non-Fungible Token)

NGFW (cortafuegos de nueva generación): NGFW (New Generation FireWall)

No disponibilidad: Unavailability

No autorizado/a (sin autorización): Unauthorized

No disponibilidad: Unavailability

No seguro/a: Insecure

Nombre de archivo: File name

Nombre de usuario: User name

Notarización: Notarization

Noticia falsa (noticia engañosa): Fake news

Nube: Cloud

Nuke (ataque): Nuke

Nukear (realizar un ataque): To nuke

Número aleatorio: Random number

Número de identificación personal (PIN): Personal identification number (PIN)

O

Objetivo de la infección: Target of infection

Obtener acceso: To get access

Ocultación: Hiding

Ocultación de datos: Data hiding

Ocultar: To hide

Oculto/a: Hidden

Ofuscación: Obfuscation

OIM (Oferta Inicial de Moneda): ICO (Initial Coin Offering)

Oportunidad: Opportunity

Ordenador (computador/a, equipo): Computer

Ordenador personal (PC): Personal computer (PC)

Origen de datos: Data source (data origin)

OSI (interconexión de sistemas abiertos): OSI (Open Systems Interconnection)

OSINT (inteligencia de fuentes abiertas): OSINT (Open Source INTelligence)

OTP (contraseña de un solo uso): OTP (One-Time Password)

Overlay (ataque de superposición): Overlay (overlay attack)

P

P2P (Peer-to-Peer, de igual a igual): P2P (Peer-to-Peer)

P3P (plataforma para preferencias de privacidad): P3P (Platform for Privacy Preferences)

Pagos P2P: P2P payments

Paquete: Package (packet)

Paquetes de malware: Malware packages

Parche: Patch

Patrón oscuro: Dark pattern

PCI DSS (estándar de seguridad de datos para la industria de tarjetas de pago): PCI DSS (Payment Card Industry Data Security Standard)

PCN (Plan de Continuidad de Negocio): BCP (Business Continuity Plan)

PDS (Plan Director de Seguridad): SMP (Security Master Plan)

Peligro (riesgo): Hazard

Penetración (intrusión informática): Penetration

Pérdida de datos: Data loss

Perjudicial: Harmful

Pez (pececillo): Fish (minnow)

PFS (confidencialidad directa total): PFS (Perfect Forward Secrecy)

PGP (privacidad bastante buena): PGP (Pretty Good Privacy)

Pharming (ciberataque donde se manipula el tráfico de un sitio web): Pharming (malicious code to direct victims to spoofed websites)

Phisher (suplantador de identidad): Phisher

Phishing (suplantación de identidad): Phishing

Phishing por SMS (smishing): SMS phishing (smishing)

Phishing por voz (vishing): Voice phishing (vishing)

PII (información de identificación personal): PII (Personally Identifiable Information)

PIN (número de identificación personal): PIN (Personal Identification Number)

Pinchazo telefónico (escucha telefónica): Phone tapping

Pirata informático/a: Software pirate (hacker)

Piratería: Piracy

Piratería en línea (piratería informática): Online piracy

Piratería social (ingeniería social): Social engineering

Pista (seguimiento): Track

PKD (directorio de claves públicas): PKD (Public Key Directory)

Plan de continuidad de negocio (PCN): Business continuity plan (BCP)

Plan de recuperación de desastres (PRD): Disaster recovery plan (DRP)

Plan director de seguridad (PDS): Security master plan (SMP)

Plataforma de cambio descentralizada (DEX): Decentralized Exchange (DEX)

Plataforma para preferencias de privacidad (P3P): Platform for privacy preferences (P3P)

PoC (prueba de concepto): PoC (Proof of Concept)

Poisoning (envenenamiento): Poisoning

Polialfabético/a: Polyalphabetic

Poligráfico/a: Polygraphic

Poligrama: Polygram

Polimórfico/a: Polymorphic

Polimorfismo: Polymorphism

Política: Policy

Política de autenticación: Authentication policy

Política de certificados: Certificate policy

Política de contraseñas: Password policy

Política de privacidad: Privacy policy

Política de seguridad: Security policy

Poner en la lista negra: To black list

PoS (prueba de participación): PoS (Proof of Stake)

PoW (prueba de trabajo): PoW (Proof of Work)

PRD (Plan de Recuperación de Desastres): DRP (Disaster Recovery Plan)

Presionar: To press

Prevención: Prevention

Prevención de pérdida de datos (DLP): Data loss prevention (DLP)

Privacidad: Privacy

Privacidad bastante buena (PGP): Pretty good privacy (PGP)

Problema de la mochila (KP): Knapsack problem (KP)

Proceso de malware: Malware process

Process ghosting (ataque de manipulación de imágenes ejecutables): Process ghosting (executable image altering attack)

Programa de broma: Joke program

Programa de validación de algoritmos criptográficos (CAVP): Cryptographic algorithm validation program (CAVP)

Programa espía (software espía): Spyware

Propagación: Propagation

Propagar: To spread

Protección: Protection

Protección contra ataques dirigidos (TAP): Targeted attack protection (TAP)

Protección contra vulnerabilidades: Exploit protection

Protección de acceso a redes (NAP): Network access protection (NAP)

Protección insuficiente: Underprotection

Proveedor: Provider

Proveedor de servicios de seguridad gestionados: Managed security service provider (MSSP)

Prueba (test, comprobación, demostración): Test (testing, proof)

Prueba de CAPTCHA: CAPTCHA test

Prueba de penetración (prueba de intrusión): Penetration testing (pen test)

Pseudoaleatorio/a: Pseudorandom

Pseudonimización: Pseudonymization

Publicidad: Advertising

Publicidad malintencionada: Malvertising

Puerta de captura (trampa): Trapdoor

Pulsación de tecla: Keystroke

Pulverización de contraseñas: Password spraying

Puntuar: To score

Q

Qrishing (ataque de phishing a través de códigos QR)   Qrishing (phishing attack through QR codes)

QS (criba cuadrática)   QS (Quadratic Sieve)

Quitar (eliminar)   To remove

R

RaaS (ransomware como servicio): RaaS (Ransomware as a Service)

Ransomware (malware de rescate): Ransomware

Ransomware como servicio (RaaS): Ransomware as a service (RaaS)

RAT (troyano de acceso remoto): RAT (Remote Access Trojan)

Realizar el seguimiento: To keep track

Reconocimiento de voz: Voice recognition

Reconocimiento del habla: Speech recognition

Reconocimiento facial: Face recognition

Recopilación de datos: Data collection

Recopilar (recabar): To collect

Recuperación: Recovery

Recuperación automática (autorrecuperación): Automatic recovery

Recuperación de clave: Key recovery

Red: Network

Red adversaria generativa (GAN): Generative adversarial network (GAN)

Red de área local (LAN): Local area network (LAN)

Red de área extensa (WAN): Wide area network (WAN)

Red de robots (botnet): Robot network (botnet)

Red privada virtual (VPN): Virtual private network (VPN)

Red trampa: Honeynet (honey net)

Red virtual: Virtual network

Reenviar: To forward

Reforzar (fortalecer): Strengthen

Registrador de teclas (registrador de pulsaciones de teclas): Keylogger

Registro de pulsaciones de teclas: Keylogging (keystroke logging, keyboard capturing)

Reiniciar: To restart

Remitente: Sender

Remitente bloqueado: Blocked sender

Remitente desconocido: Unknown sender

Remitente falsificado (remitente suplantado): Spoofed sender

Relleno de credenciales: Credential stuffing

Relleno de píxeles Pixel stuffing

Rescate: Ransom

Respuesta a incidentes: Incident response

Restricción: Restriction

Retrovirus: Retrovirus

RFID (identificación por radiofrecuencia): RFID (Radio Frequency Identification)

RGPD (Reglamento General de Protección de Datos): GDPR (General Data Protection Regulation)

Riesgo: Risk

Robo de datos: Data theft

Robo de identidad: Identity theft

Rogueware (software malicioso que hace creer que hay un virus en el sistema): Rogueware (malicious software that misleads users into believing there is a virus on their computer)

Rooting (rooteo): Rooting

Rootkit (software malicioso): Rootkit (malicious software)

RSA (Rivest, Shamir y Adleman, sistema criptográfico de clave pública): RSA (Rivest-Shamir-Adleman, public key encryption method)

S

Sabotaje (cibersabotaje): Sabotage (cybersabotage)

SAC (criterio estricto de avalancha): SAC (Strict Avalanche Criterion)

Salvaguardar (proteger): To safeguard

Sandbox (entorno de pruebas aislado): Sandbox

SCADA (control de supervisión y adquisición de datos): SCADA (Supervisory Control and Data Acquisition)

Scareware (malware para asustar): Scareware

SCI (Sistema de Control Industrial): ICS (Industrial Control System)

Secuestrador: Hijacker

Secuestrar: To hijack

Secuestro: Hijacking

Secuestro de datos (ransomware, malware de rescate): Ransomware

Seguimiento: Tracking

Seguridad: Security (safety)

Seguridad de la capa de transporte (TLS): Transport layer security (TLS)

Seguridad de la información: Information security

Seguridad de red: Network security

Seguro/a: Secure

Sello de confianza: Trust mark

Sello de tiempo (marca de tiempo): Timestamp

Sensible (confidencial): Sensitive

Señuelo: Decoy

SET (transacción electronica segura): SET (Secure Electronic Transaction)

Sexting (envío de contenido sexual): Sexting (sex messaging)

Sextorsión (extorsión sexual): Sextorsion (sexual extorsion)

SFTP (protocolo transferencia segura de archivos): SFTP (Secure File Transfer Protocol)

SGSI (Sistema de Gestión de la Seguridad de la Información): ISMS (Information Security Management System)

Shallowfake (cheapfake, técnicas básicas de edición de vídeo para crear engaños): Shallowfake (cheapfake, fake media produced using easily available and cheap tools)

SIEM (administración de eventos e información de seguridad): SIEM (Security Information and Event Management)

Sigiloso/a (oculto/a, furtivo/a): Stealth

Sin autorización: Unauthorized

Sistema abierto: Open system

Sistema comprometido: Compromised system

Sistema criptográfico: Cryptograhic system

Sistema de detección de intrusos (IDS): Intrusion detection system (IDS)

Sistema de prevención de intrusos (IPS): Intrusion prevention system (IPS)

Sitio web fraudulento: Fraudulent website

Skimmer (dispositivo que copia de tarjetas de crédito): Skimmer (device that copies credit cards)

Skimming (fraude a las tarjetas bancarias y números PIN): Skimming (theft of credit and debit card data and PIN numbers)

Smishing (phishing por SMS): Smishing (SMS phishing)

Sniffer (husmeador, rastreador): Sniffer

Sniffing (captura de tráfico de red): Sniffing

SOC (centro de operaciones de seguridad): SOC (Security Operations Center)

Software (programa): Software

Software antiespía: Antispyware

Software espía: Spyware

Software de detección de virus: Virus detection software

Software falsificado: Counterfeit software

Software malicioso (malware): Malicious software (malware)

Software publicitario: Adware

Sospechoso/a: Suspicious

Spam (correo no deseado, correo basura): Spam

Spammer (emisor/a de correo basura): Spammer (person who sends spam)

Spamming (envío masivo de correo basura, inundación): Spamming (sending of multiple unsolicited emails or text messages)

Spoofing (suplantación de identidad): Spoofing

Spyware (software espía, programa espía): Spyware

SSH (shell seguro): SSH (Secure Shell)

SSID (identificador de conjunto de servicios): SSID (Service Set Identifier)

SSL (capa de sockets seguros): SSL (Secure Sockets Layer)

Subida (carga): Upload

Subir (cargar): To upload

Supercifrado: Superencryption (superencipherment)

Suplantación de identidad: Spoofing (impersonation, identity theft)

Suplantado/a: Spoofed

Suplantar: To spoof

T

Tabla de seguimiento: Trace table

Tailgating (piggybacking): Tailgating (piggybacking)

TAP (protección contra ataques dirigidos): TAP (Targeted Attack Protection)

Tarjeta: Card

Tarjeta bancaria: Bank card

Tarjeta magnética: Magnetic card

Tasa de rechazo erróneo (FRR): False rejection rate (FRR)

Tecla: Key

Teclado: Keyboard

Técnica de hackeo: Hacking technique

Técnicas de descifrado de contraseñas: Password cracking techniques

Teléfono: Phone (telephone)

Tercero de confianza (TTP): Trusted third party (TTP)

Texto incomprensible (texto codificado): Garbled text

Tiempo de instalación (tiempo de preparación): Setup time

Tienda en línea (tienda online, tienda virtual): Online store

Timar (estafar, engañar): To swindle (to scam, to cheat)

Timador/a (estafador/a): Swindler (scammer, hustler, diddler)

Timo (estafa, engaño, fraude): Swindle (scam, fraud)

Tirón de alfombra: Rug pull

Token (ficha, criptovalor): Token

Token de seguridad: Security token

Token de utilidad: Utility token

Token no fungible (NFT): Non-fungible token (NFT)

Tokenización de activos: Asset tokenization

TPM (módulo de plataforma segura): TPM (Trusted Platform Module)

Tráfico: Traffic

Tráfico de paquetes: Packet traffic

Tráfico de red: Network traffic

Tráfico de red sospechoso: Suspicious network traffic

Transacción electronica segura (SET): Secure electronic transaction (SET)

Transferencia bancaria: Bank transfer (wire transfer)

Transferencia inconsciente: Oblivious transfer

Transferir: To transfer

Transparencia: Transparency

Traza (seguimiento): Trace

Trazabilidad: Traceability

Triple extorsión: Triple extorsion

Troyano: Trojan

Troyano de acceso remoto (RAT): Remote access trojan (RAT)

Troyano dropper (troyano cuentagotas): Trojan dropper

TLS (seguridad de la capa de transporte): TLS (Transport Layer Security)

U

UI (interfaz de usuario, IU): UI (User Interface)

Unidad de crímenes digitales (DCU): Digital crime unit (DCU)

URL (localizador uniforme de recursos): URL (Uniform Resouce Locator)

USB (bus serie universal): USB (Universal Serial Bus)

USB malicioso (BadUSB): BadUSB (Rubber Ducky, bad beetle USB)

Uso indebido: Misuse

Usuario anónimo: Anonymous user

Usuario autorizado: Authorized user

Usuario con identidad suplantada: Spoofed user

Usuario fantasma: Ghost user

Usuario malintencionado: Malicious user

Usuario no autorizado: Unauthorized user

Usurpación de identidad: Identity fraud

Utility token (token de utilidad): Utility token

V

VA (autoridad de validación): VA (Validation Authority)

Vaciado: Hollowing

Vacuna de ciberseguridad: Cybersecurity vaccine

Validación de datos: Data validation

Variante de malware: Malware variant

Variante de virus: Virus variant

Vector de ataque: Attack vector

Ventanización: Windowing

Verdadero/a: True

Verificación de huella digital: Fingerprint verification

Verificación facial: Face verification

Víctima: Victim

Víctima de un fraude: Victim of fraud

Victimizar: To victimize

Videovigilancia (vigilancia por vídeo): Video surveillance

Violación (infracción, vulneración): Violation (infringement, breach)

Violación de seguridad: Security violation

Virtualización: Virtualization

Virus: Virus

Virus cifrado: Encrypted virus

Virus de archivo ejecutable: Executable file virus

Virus de sobreescritura: Overwriting virus

Virus ejecutable: Executable virus

Virus engañoso (virus fraudulento): Hoax virus (hoaxing virus)

Virus informático: Computer virus

Virus latente: Sleeping virus

Virus oculto (virus furtivo): Stealth virus

Vishing (phishing por voz): Vishing (voice phishing, VoIP phishing)

Vista de árbol: Tree view

Volatilidad: Volatility

VPN (red privada virtual): VPN (Virtual Private Network)

Vulnerabilidad: Vulnerability

Vulnerabilidad de día cero: Zero-day (O-day)

Vulnerabilidad del producto: Product vulnerability

Vulnerabilidades y exposiciones comunes (CVE): Common vulnerabilities and exposures (CVE)

Vulneración (infracción, violación): Breach

Vulneración de datos: Data breach

W

WAN (red de área extensa): WAN (wide area network)

Web oscura (Internet oscura, dark web): Dark web

Web profunda (Internet profunda): Deep web

Web visible: Surface web

WEP (privacidad equivalente a cableado): WEP (Wired Equivalent Privacy)

WWW (telaraña mundial): WWW (World Wide Web)

X

XMR (monero, criptomoneda de código abierto): XMR (monero, open-source cryptocurrency)

XSS (scripting entre sitios): XSS (Cross Site Scripting)

Z

Zero-party data (datos declarados): Zero-party data (declared data)

ZKP (prueba de conocimiento nulo): ZKP (Zero Knowledge Proof)

Zombi (dispositivo infectado por malware y que está controlado por un hacker): Zombie (device infected with malware that is controlled by a hacker)

Zona de seguridad: Security zone

Zona desmilitarizada (DMZ): Demilitarized zone (DMZ)

Zoombombing (asalto de videoconferencia): Zoombombing (videoconference bombing)

www.ingramcontent.com/pod-product-compliance
Lightning Source LLC
LaVergne TN
LVHW051744050326
832903LV00029B/2711